BE
CONFIDENT

T0343585

BE CONFIDENT

An Hachette UK Company
www.hachette.co.uk

Vie Books, an imprint of Summersdale Publishers
Part of Octopus Publishing Group Limited
Carmelite House
50 Victoria Embankment
LONDON
EC4Y 0DZ
UK

www.summersdale.com

Printed and bound in Poland

ISBN: 978-1-83799-455-7

This FSC® label means that materials used for the product have been responsibly sourced

MIX
Paper | Supporting responsible forestry
FSC® C018236

Substantial discounts on bulk quantities of Summersdale books are available to corporations, professional associations and other organizations. For details contact general enquiries: telephone: +44 (0) 1243 771107 or email: enquiries@summersdale.com.

Disclaimer
Neither the author nor the publisher can be held responsible for any loss, damage or injury – be it health, financial or otherwise – arising out of the use, or misuse, of the suggestions made herein.

BE CONFIDENT

A Child's Guide to Conquering Fears

Poppy O'Neill

CONTENTS

Foreword...7

Introduction: A guide for parents and carers.....................8

How to use this book: A guide for children.....................11

Introducing Buzz the monster..12

PART 1: CONFIDENCE AND ME.....................................13

All about me..14

My life house..16

What is confidence?..18

Activity: I feel confident when…...........................20

What does high confidence feel like for me?........23

What does low confidence feel like for me?.........24

Help Buzz build confidence...................................25

Activity: Make a confidence collage!....................27

PART 2: HOW TO BE CONFIDENT..............................31

How does confidence work?.................................32

Building a confidence staircase...........................33

Going at your own pace.......................................37

Challenging yourself..39

Who can I talk to?..40

Activity: Build your confidence staircase............42

Keep a confidence tracker...................................43

Activity: Finding bravery.....................................46

Practice makes progress......................................48

How you talk to yourself matters.......................50

Swapping negative self-talk for positive self-talk.........52

PART 3: IT'S OK TO BE MYSELF 57

We are all unique..58

Expressing emotions...59

Helping our emotions to move...61

Activity: My strengths..63

I like myself! 64

Activity: One step at a time...66

Activity: Confident colouring...68

Saying no..70

Your secret superpower..72

Making mistakes..76

Activity: Scribble magic!..77

My most confident self..79

It's OK to feel how you feel..82

Activity: Help Buzz get creative.......................................83

PART 4: LOOKING AFTER YOU 84

Why is taking care of ourselves important for confidence?.......85

Confidence-building food...86

Home-made pitta pizza..87

Frozen yoghurt bites..88

Fluffy banana breakfast pancakes.....................................89

Confidence and sleep..90

Activity: Move your body!...91

Go wild..95

Make a nature mandala..96

Making time to chill out...98

Confidence-building friendships.......................................100

What makes a good friend?...101

Activity: My good friend...103

Building confidence together..104

Activity: Building independence...106
Building body confidence...110
Feed your mind good things...111

PART 5: QUICK CONFIDENCE BOOSTERS........................113

Breathing in confidence..114
Activity: My confidence file...117
How gratitude boosts confidence.....................................120
Activity: Gratitude challenges!.......................................121
Shaking off anxiety...123
Speak yourself confident..125
The best that can happen...127

PART 6: LOOKING FORWARD...................................129

Golden rules for confidence...130
You are not alone...131
Spreading ripples of confidence.....................................133
Activity: Make a confidence-building poster....................134
The end..137

For parents and carers: Ways you can support your child's confidence........139
Further advice...140
Recommended reading..141

FOREWORD

Mayvrill Freeston-Roberts
Counsellor, Psychotherapist, Qualified Clinical Supervisor,
registered and accredited by the British Association
for Counselling and Psychotherapy

Be Confident offers useful approaches to help children understand their feelings in numerous ways, primarily by helping them to build confidence in themselves and grow their self-belief. Buzz the friendly monster enables the young reader, through wise and achievable exercises, to conquer their fears and promotes a "can do" approach with kindness, fun and encouragement.

The book boasts a wealth of interactive activities, helping young readers achieve healthy levels of self-belief as they excel in the enjoyable exercises and work towards building self-confidence. The practical skills Buzz shares look to enhance every child's ability to have faith in themselves, and the engaging exercises will help children discover how to become free from anxieties and self-sabotaging beliefs.

Be Confident, helps children to understand emotions and recognize feelings as part of being a healthy person. Furthermore, it makes clear that most people share the same doubts and fears, and as Buzz recommends; by being brave and facing challenges we can achieve amazing things, or, just as usefully, learn what may work better next time.

As a parent, grandparent and great-grandparent, I regard myself as fortunate to have raised my three confident, capable children, even though I myself was hampered by a lack of confidence well into adulthood. If I had had such a brilliant book as *Be Confident* as a child, it would have helped me to believe in myself and my abilities much earlier.

I fully endorse this wonderful book as an effective guide to enhance a child's confidence and overall development. It provides insightful guidance for parents, caregivers, and children alike.

INTRODUCTION:
A GUIDE FOR PARENTS AND CARERS

Be Confident is a practical guide designed to engage children with their inner confidence and overcome self-doubt. With the help of activities and ideas based on techniques developed by child psychologists, this book aims to support your child in understanding their emotions better, enabling them to build tools to increase their confidence.

We often think about people being naturally confident, and while for some this may be the case, for most people it's more complex and acting with confidence involves some measure of bravery. On the outside, it can seem as though others take life's challenges in their stride, so it's really important to accept that feelings of anxiety, nervousness and self-doubt are completely normal, rather than a sign that your child should avoid the challenge they are facing.

Maybe your child is having a hard time making friends or feels unable to ask for help when they need it. Perhaps their confidence has taken a knock and you're looking for ways to support them as they rebuild it. The thing about confidence is, having someone on your team – an understanding, compassionate, trusted adult – can make all the difference.

This book is for children aged 7–11 – an age when they might begin to feel self-conscious, might compare themselves to others and might start to develop more complex friendships. Add to that the first signs of puberty and new pressures at school, and it makes sense that confidence can take a tumble around this time. If this sounds like your child, you're not alone. With your patience, support and understanding, they can find their inner confidence, build up their resilience and confidently be themselves.

Here are some of the main signs that low confidence could be holding your child back:

- Reluctance to try new things

- Difficulty speaking up for themselves

- Being very hard on themselves

- Strong emotional reactions when they make a mistake

- Perfectionism

- Seeking approval and reassurance frequently

- Apologizing often, even when they've done nothing wrong

It can be useful to keep a diary of your child's behaviour – doing so can help shed light on patterns you might not otherwise notice, bringing you a better understanding of your child.

It can be really challenging to look at our children's mental and emotional health – occasionally, we as parents and carers might identify ways in which our own behaviour, while well-intentioned, has been unhelpful. Be kind to yourself and remember that you are giving your child an incredible gift by taking an interest in and supporting their emotional development. Confidence is best thought of as a habit rather than something we either have or don't have, and that means it's never too late to start developing it.

How to use this book:
For parents and carers

This book is for your child, so it's best to let them take the lead when it comes to helping them read through it. Some children might be happy working on the activities independently, while others might benefit from a little guidance and encouragement. Letting your child set the pace is one small way you can help them build confidence.

However your child approaches this book, it's a great idea to show an active interest and start a conversation around it. Ask your child about what they've learned or realized, or any parts they've found unhelpful or boring – sharing their thoughts and feelings openly is a really important part of building confidence, so use this book as a tool for honest feedback.

The activities are designed to get your child thinking about the way their emotions and minds work, so let them know that there are no wrong answers and that they are the expert on how they feel inside. Hopefully this book will help your child understand themselves better and increase their sense of self-confidence. If you have any serious concerns about your child's mental health, however, your doctor is the best person to go to for further advice.

HOW TO USE THIS BOOK: A GUIDE FOR CHILDREN

What does it mean to be confident? You might think confidence is all about never feeling worried or making a mistake. You might think people are either confident or they aren't. This book will show you that there's a lot more to confidence than meets the eye!

When we don't feel confident, it can have a big effect on us. Here are a few signs that low confidence might be causing you trouble:

You hold back from trying new things.

You often feel like others are better than you.

You think things will go badly, so you play it safe.

You find it hard to ask for help when you need it.

If that sounds like you some of the time, or even most of the time, you're not alone. Lots of kids struggle with their confidence levels, but they don't always show it on the outside. This book is here to help you find the confidence that's already inside you, while still being yourself.

Keep reading to find lots of fun activities, interesting ideas and tips to help you try new things, learn all about your thoughts and feelings, and grow your confidence. You can read through the book at your own pace. If there's anything you want to share or ask about, you can talk to your grown-up at any point.

INTRODUCING BUZZ THE MONSTER

Hello! It's great to see you – I'm Buzz, and I'm here to guide you through this book. Inside, you'll find so many things to do and exciting ideas to learn about. I can't wait to get started. Are you ready? Then let's begin.

PART 1:
CONFIDENCE AND ME

In this chapter, we'll be learning all about you and all about confidence. Getting to know yourself and how confidence works for you is a really important step towards conquering your fears.

ALL ABOUT ME

Can you write in the shapes to help Buzz get to know you better?

My name is...

I am __ years old.

I'm good at...

I'm looking forward to...

My favourite part of the day is...

My favourite
food is...

My least favourite
food is...

I'm a good
friend when...

I feel great
when I wear...

The best book I've
ever read is...

MY LIFE HOUSE

Can you decorate this house to show some of the parts of your life? Draw or write your ideas in the spaces.

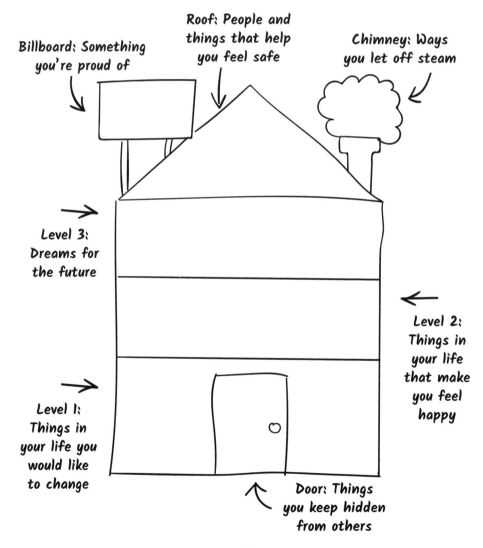

Billboard: Something you're proud of

Roof: People and things that help you feel safe

Chimney: Ways you let off steam

Level 3: Dreams for the future

Level 2: Things in your life that make you feel happy

Level 1: Things in your life you would like to change

Door: Things you keep hidden from others

Who or what brings sunshine and happiness into your life

People or things that make you feel stormy, angry or upset

WHAT IS CONFIDENCE?

Confidence means feeling sure of yourself and your abilities. Who is the most confident person you can think of? It's probably someone who's really good at what they do, perhaps someone who does difficult things but makes them look easy. The truth is, everybody has different levels of confidence about different things. Let's explore this idea…

A famous singer may feel very confident performing on stage, but when they were just starting out, they had to build confidence just like they had to learn the words of their songs and the moves to their dance routines.

That same famous singer is bound to have things in their life they don't feel confident about – it could be ice skating, drawing or making friends.

Confidence is a feeling that grows as we build skills. It doesn't happen by magic, though it may come more easily to some people than others.

If that all sounds like a lot of hard work, here's some good news: there are lots of ways you can make building confidence easier for yourself. That's what this book is all about!

I CAN
TRY NEW
THINGS

ACTIVITY: I FEEL CONFIDENT WHEN...

Think about some skills you've practised and feel confident about. It could be drawing a particular character, riding a bike or scooter, singing a song you know all the words to…

Write or draw your confident skills here:

I feel confident when I...

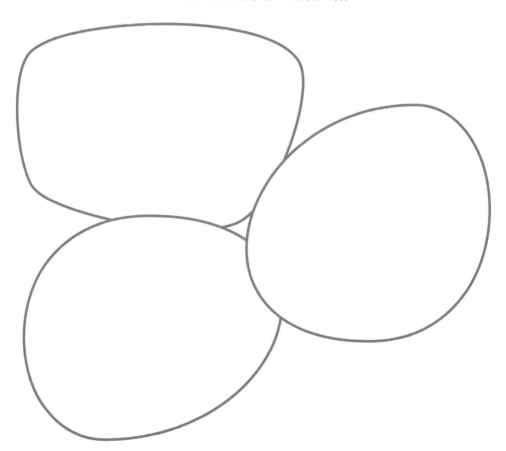

Now have a think about the things you're learning but don't yet feel very confident about. It could be a subject at school, a dance routine, a recipe… Write or draw your ideas in the shapes below.

I'm building confidence in...

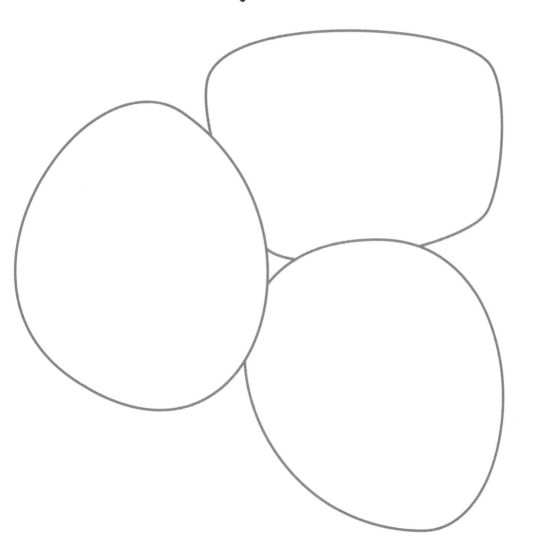

Lastly, let's think about some totally new skills that you haven't tried yet. These might be activities you'd love to do, a challenge coming up that you're feeling nervous about or just something that feels both scary and exciting that you'd like to experience in the future. Write or draw about them here.

I'd like to build the confidence to try...

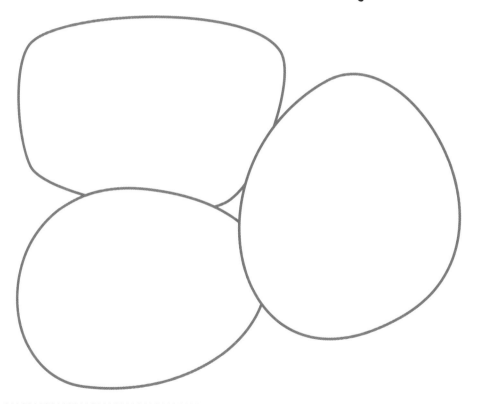

Thinking about skills and challenges as things we're building confidence in – rather than things we are good or bad at – helps us see that, with a little hard work and dedication, it's possible to feel confident about anything!

WHAT DOES HIGH CONFIDENCE FEEL LIKE FOR ME?

Think back to page 20 and pick one thing you feel confident about right now. Close your eyes and imagine you are confidently doing that thing – look at you go! How do you feel when your confidence levels are high? Draw a circle around the words that fit – and add your own ideas if you like.

Excited

Happy

Joyful

Serious

Focused

Powerful

Bubbly

Scared

Calm

Lost in the moment

Tired

WHAT DOES LOW CONFIDENCE FEEL LIKE FOR ME?

When we're low on confidence, it can feel really uncomfortable. Doing something that feels like a big challenge is really hard – especially if there are others around who appear more confident. Everybody feels low confidence in different ways – here's how some other kids have described feeling this way:

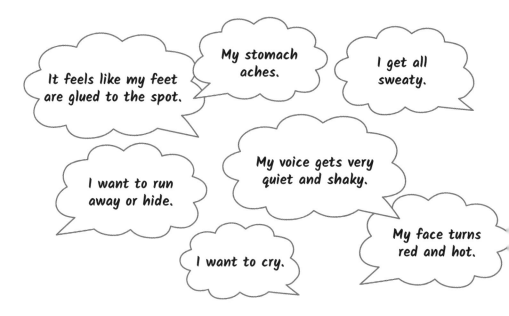

It feels like my feet are glued to the spot.

My stomach aches.

I get all sweaty.

I want to run away or hide.

My voice gets very quiet and shaky.

My face turns red and hot.

I want to cry.

Do you feel any of these feelings when you're faced with a challenge and your confidence levels are low? Colour any of these bubbles blue.

It's OK to find some things really challenging, even if it seems like no big deal to others. Some days, it takes a lot of bravery to do your best.

HELP BUZZ BUILD CONFIDENCE

Buzz feels very low in confidence when it's time to go into the lunch hall. It's very loud and busy, and Buzz is worried there won't be any friends to sit with. Buzz is standing outside the lunch hall, thinking:

Everybody else is good at going into the lunch hall. It's easy for them and they always find a friend to sit next to – I'm just bad at going into the lunch hall!

Remember that confidence is something we can build. Which of these speech bubbles might help Buzz feel better and build a little confidence? Choose one bubble and colour it in.

Which did you choose? The most helpful answer is number two! Answer number two reminds Buzz that all feelings are OK, and that with bravery and determination, confidence can be built.

ACTIVITY: MAKE A CONFIDENCE COLLAGE!

When you're working on changing the way you think and feel, it really helps to use all your senses. In this activity, we're going to create a sensory confidence collage that's totally unique. First, let's gather some ideas:

Sight
What colour makes you feel confident?

_____

_____

Hear
Which song makes you feel unstoppable?

_____

_____

Smell
What smells make you feel great?

_____

_____

Touch
What comfy clothes make you feel relaxed and ready for anything?

_____

_____

Taste
Can you think of one energy-boosting favourite fruit?

_____

_____

On the next page, you'll find space to make a confidence collage. Using the ideas you've written above, gather pictures and words from newspapers, magazines and leaflets (remember to ask your grown-up before you cut or tear any pictures) that show your ideas. If you can't find an image or text that's quite right, don't worry – why not just carefully cut the shape out of coloured paper, or simply draw it?

Stick your pictures on the following page – you can use the guidelines or make it up yourself. Keep adding to your collage until you're ready to stop – you can use as many pictures as you like for each sense.

When you need a boost of confidence, pick up this book and turn to your confidence collage – seeing it will help you feel good about yourself.

My confident colour

My confident smell

Con
Co

Stick your images onto the page using the guidelines, or let your imagination run wild – you're in charge!

My
confident
clothing

My
confident
fruit

My
confident
song

I CAN GO AT MY OWN PACE

PART 2:
HOW TO BE CONFIDENT

Now we understand what confidence is and how it feels for you, let's go deeper. In this chapter, we'll dive into how confidence works and how to build it.

HOW DOES CONFIDENCE WORK?

Our brains use information from what's happened to us before to work out how we feel about things that haven't happened yet. If every time you tried something new you did it perfectly on your first try, you'd always feel super-confident about trying new things.

The trouble is, no one is perfect at new things on their first try… or their second, third or fourth! If you've ever seen a baby learning to walk, you'll notice that they're really wobbly at first and do lots of tumbling over. One of the great things about babies is that they don't care at all whether they look a bit silly.

As we grow older, we start to worry about looking silly, and so trying something where we might wobble, make mistakes or even fail completely starts to feel pretty scary.

When something is new to us, our brains only have information about times we've tried other new things, so usually, we don't feel confident at first.

The tricky thing about confidence is that the only way to build it is by acting with bravery – and that means doing the thing you're scared to do while you're still feeling scared.

When we act with bravery, we give our brains new information, which we can use in our next try. That information gives our doubts and fears a chance to shrink and our confidence gets a chance to grow. So, the secret to building confidence is to make acting with bravery as easy as possible. Confused? Let's break it down…

BUILDING A CONFIDENCE STAIRCASE

Buzz wants to audition for the school summer production. It sounds really fun and lots of Buzz's friends are auditioning, but the audition means singing a song up on stage, and Buzz's confidence levels are low when it comes to singing on a stage.

Imagine Buzz and the audition like this:

Buzz's feelings of low confidence, nervousness and fear mean that the auditions feel almost impossible.

But what if Buzz was able to build a staircase, so the audition didn't feel so out of reach?

Using bravery, Buzz can build the confidence to audition for the summer production. By breaking that bravery down into steps, Buzz makes it easier to build confidence.

How many steps can you spot in the picture?

We use steps all the time to make it easier for us to reach things. Let's take a closer look at what Buzz's confidence staircase is made of.

Talk about my feelings with someone I trust

Watch videos of the song being performed

Practise the song at home by myself

Learn some tools to find calm and bravery (see Part 5)

Sing the song in front of trusted friends or family members

Practise being on stage

Learn the song by heart

Audition

Can you see how each step makes it that bit easier for Buzz to act with bravery? Buzz still has to climb each step, but the smaller the steps, the easier it will be to get to the top.

Whatever the challenge, finding the best steps that make your journey easier will help you build the bravery to reach your goal.

Now let's give Buzz a different challenge.

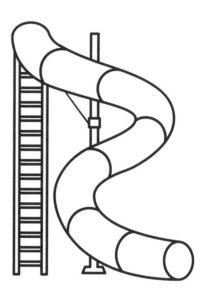

The waterslide at Buzz's local swimming pool looks so much fun and Buzz really wants to try it out! Buzz is tall enough to ride the waterslide now – the trouble is, it's very high and Buzz feels low on confidence.

How could Buzz build confidence about trying the waterslide?

Here are some suggestions to get you thinking:

Talk about their feelings with someone they trust

Ask a friend what it feels like to go down the waterslide

Go down a smaller waterslide

Ask a member of staff some questions

Have fun in the swimming pool

GOING AT YOUR OWN PACE

When building confidence, it's important to go at your own pace. If you feel rushed, usually your feelings of fear, stress and worry will go up, and your confidence levels will go down.

When you know that you can take breaks, slow down or say, "No, I'm not ready," a lot of your feelings of fear, stress and worry will get smaller.

Why not take a break now with some relaxing colouring?

CHALLENGING YOURSELF

If you're building confidence, it's important to go at your own pace and it's also important to challenge yourself. That's why small, brave steps are so useful – they keep you moving toward your goal without rushing or doing things you're not ready for.

Think about something that's a challenge for you. It might be one of the ideas you wrote down on page 21 or 22, or something else. Write your challenge here:

Whatever your challenge, one of the most important steps for building confidence is to talk about how you feel with someone you trust. Can you write about or draw how you feel here?

You could ask someone you trust to help you with this page – it will make it easier to start a conversation about how to build confidence.

WHO CAN I TALK TO?

Talking about our feelings is very powerful! When we share how we feel with someone trustworthy, we realize we are not alone with our thoughts and emotions, and that others want to understand and help us with our challenges.

Think about the person or people in your life that you feel most calm and comfortable around, and that you trust. You don't need to trust someone just because they're a grown-up or they're being kind – trust is a feeling inside you.

A trusted person might be a school friend, a brother or sister, or a grown-up. A trusted grown-up could be a parent, carer, teacher, neighbour, family member or someone else – someone who is a good listener, treats you with respect and cares about you. You might have lots of people you feel OK talking to, or maybe just one or two.

Write or draw your trusted person/people here:

I AM
NOT
ALONE

ACTIVITY:
BUILD YOUR CONFIDENCE STAIRCASE

Are you ready to build confidence? Add your goal to the top and fill in each stair with small, brave steps towards your challenge. You can do it!

My goal

Bonus: draw yourself here!

KEEP A CONFIDENCE TRACKER

Now you've worked out the steps to take that will get you to your goal, why not keep a diary so you can track your progress? Remember: it's OK to go at your own pace, repeat steps and take breaks – you're in charge.

Brave step:

How I felt before:

How I felt after:

What I learned:

I am ready (tick one below)...

☐ for the next step   ☐ for a break   ☐ to repeat this step

Brave step:

How I felt before:

How I felt after:

What I learned:

I am ready (tick one below)...

☐ for the next step   ☐ for a break   ☐ to repeat this step

Brave step:

How I felt before:

How I felt after:

What I learned:

I am ready (tick one below)...

☐ for the next step   ☐ for a break   ☐ to repeat this step

Brave step:

How I felt before:

How I felt after:

What I learned:

I am ready (tick one below)...

☐ for the next step   ☐ for a break   ☐ to repeat this step

Brave step:

How I felt before:

How I felt after:

What I learned:

I am ready (tick one below)...

☐ for the next step   ☐ for a break   ☐ to repeat this step

Brave step:

How I felt before:

How I felt after:

What I learned:

I am ready (tick one below)...

☐ for the next step   ☐ for a break   ☐ to repeat this step

Brave step:

How I felt before:

How I felt after:

What I learned:

I am ready (tick one below)...

☐ for the next step   ☐ for a break   ☐ to repeat this step

Brave step:

How I felt before:

How I felt after:

What I learned:

I am ready (tick one below)...

☐ for the next step   ☐ for a break   ☐ to repeat this step

ACTIVITY: FINDING BRAVERY

We've learned that the trickiest part of building confidence is finding the bravery to take the next step. We all have bravery within us, but sometimes it's hard to find. Let's look at some ways to find the bravery you need.

Stand tall

When you move your body like someone very brave, it becomes easier to *be* someone very brave!

Try this now:

- Stand up, with your head high, shoulders relaxed and feet slightly apart.

- Place your hands on your hips.

- Take a deep breath.

- Look out of a window to the sky or horizon.

What do you notice about how standing like this makes you feel? Write your ideas here:

Speak yourself brave

Imagine you have a fairy godmother, sports coach or mentor who's always there to give you a confidence-boosting pep talk. You can be a mentor for yourself! Try this now:

Stand in front of a mirror or close your eyes and put your hand on your heart – however feels most comfortable to talk to yourself. Say these words to yourself, out loud or in your head:

I am brave.

I can do this.

I can do hard things.

I will be kind to myself, no matter what.

I can go at my own pace.

I am always learning and growing.

I am always doing my best.

What do you notice about how saying these words makes you feel? Write your ideas here:

It might seem strange to stand or talk like you are feeling brave if you aren't. You don't need to hide how you really feel in order to be brave. But making changes to how you speak and move your body will help shift your feelings towards bravery and make it that much easier to face challenges with confidence.

PRACTICE MAKES PROGRESS

Each time you practise, you learn a little more about the skill or goal you're aiming for. That's why messing up, being imperfect and making mistakes is really valuable – you learn what works well by also learning what doesn't work so well.

Can you think of some of the skills and goals you've practised and mastered in your life? Write or draw them here!

Talking: Which language or languages do you speak?

Writing: Write your name in your best handwriting!

Reading: Which books do you like to read?

Singing: Sing a song you know by heart.

Playing: Write the rules of a game you love.

HOW YOU TALK TO YOURSELF MATTERS

Remember on page 47 when we tried speaking bravely to help ourselves feel confident? The way we think and talk about ourselves is a big part of how confident we feel. One of the ways we might accidentally lower our own confidence is with something called negative self-talk.

Negative self-talk means being unkind to yourself in your mind, and in the way you speak about yourself to others. Negative self-talk can have a huge effect on confidence levels. Here's why:

Buzz is about to start learning a new skill: how to play the guitar. But hang on a minute… Buzz's brain is being unkind!

How do you think Buzz is feeling about learning guitar?

Buzz is feeling pretty low in confidence, and those unkind thoughts are making it worse!

The good news is that self-talk can also be positive. Let's see what a difference positive self-talk can make:

How might Buzz be feeling this time?

_____

_____

Did you notice that in both pictures, Buzz's skill at playing guitar is the same, but with positive self-talk, it was a lot easier for Buzz to feel confident and start practising? That's why it's so powerful! Let's learn how to swap negative self-talk for positive self-talk.

SWAPPING NEGATIVE SELF-TALK FOR POSITIVE SELF-TALK

We all have self-talk. Without thinking about it or trying, we have thoughts or feelings about ourselves, just like we have thoughts and feelings about the things other people do and say.

Talking to yourself with kindness rather than being your own bully sounds simple, but it can be tricky! It might feel strange at first, but like any skill, the more you practise, the easier it gets.

Kind, confident self-talk doesn't mean thinking "I am the greatest and best person ever!", it means showing yourself understanding, patience and friendliness – especially when you're feeling upset, worried or low on confidence. Here's an example:

Positive self-talk says:
That's OK, everyone makes mistakes – let's try again.

Negative self-talk says:
Throw your work in the bin, you'll never get this right.

I made a mistake on my schoolwork

Even if our first thoughts are negative self-talk, we can make a choice to think kind, positive thoughts too.

Try it yourself!

Below you'll find some situations that lots of people find tricky. Can you draw a line to connect the positive self-talk to each situation?

It's my turn to read aloud in class.

Ouch, that felt embarrassing. I'm OK – it happens to everyone.

I'm meeting my friend but they're late.

If I show kindness and be myself, I'll make good friends.

I made a spelling mistake.

I've forgotten something – I can tell the truth and put it right.

I forgot to do my homework.

I feel nervous. I'll take a deep breath and do my best.

I'd like to make a new friend.

I wonder what's keeping them? I'm sure they'll be here soon.

I tripped over at the park.

That's OK, mistakes are a brilliant way to learn.

Now you've learned all about positive self-talk, can you help Buzz again?

Buzz is enjoying learning to play the guitar but is having trouble mastering this song. Buzz can't quite get the beginning to sound right.

Can you think of some positive self-talk for Buzz? Write your ideas in the thought bubble!

When we're building confidence, learning new skills and acting with bravery, there will be challenges, mistakes and setbacks along the way – that's just life! The tips and ideas in this book won't stop tricky things from happening, but they will give you tools for being on your own team, finding your bravery and trying again.

Learning the skill of positive self-talk means that even when things don't go your way, you'll always have a kind, encouraging friend in yourself – and that's where true confidence comes from.

I AM ALWAYS LEARNING AND GROWING

PART 3:
IT'S OK TO BE MYSELF

When your aim is to build up confidence, it can feel like you need to change into a different sort of person: a confident person. But that's not the case. When you're truly confident, you feel comfortable being yourself even when facing a challenge. In this chapter, we'll learn all about emotions and how they help you be your most confident self.

WE ARE ALL UNIQUE

Each person is made up of lots of qualities – their likes and dislikes, memories, family, experiences, thoughts, feelings, how much milk they have on their cereal… These qualities make a person themselves, and each one of us is totally unique! At the same time, we have lots in common with one another. Confidence is a quality we all have within us, but we show it on the outside in different ways. If you ask someone what confidence is like for them, they'll probably be able to tell you their unique way of experiencing it.

"I feel pretty confident most of the time. Trying new things doesn't bother me. The one thing that I really struggle with is going to the dentist."

"Confidence is tricky for me. It's like there's a voice in my head telling me things are going to go wrong, so feeling confident is hard."

"Maths is my best subject and I feel confident about it – even when I'm learning something new. I don't feel confident about sport, though – not at all!"

EXPRESSING EMOTIONS

Everybody feels emotions, and we all show them differently on the outside. One person might be feeling really worried on the inside and show that worry through their face, behaviour or by speaking about their feelings, while another might be feeling just as worried but not show it at all on the outside.

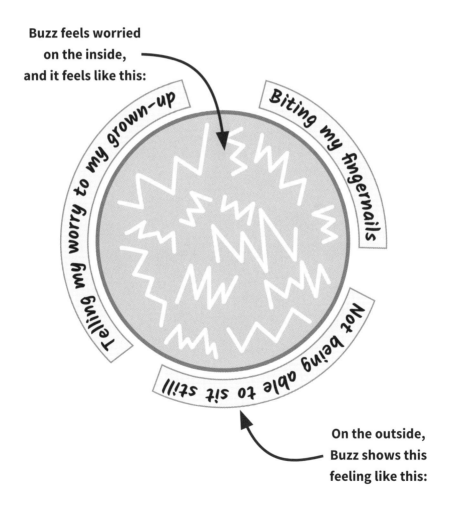

Buzz feels worried on the inside, and it feels like this:

Telling my worry to my grown-up

Biting my fingernails

Not being able to sit still

On the outside, Buzz shows this feeling like this:

Now you try – how does worry feel to you? Draw or write about it in the circle.

How do you show your worry on the outside? Write your ideas in the shapes outside the circle.

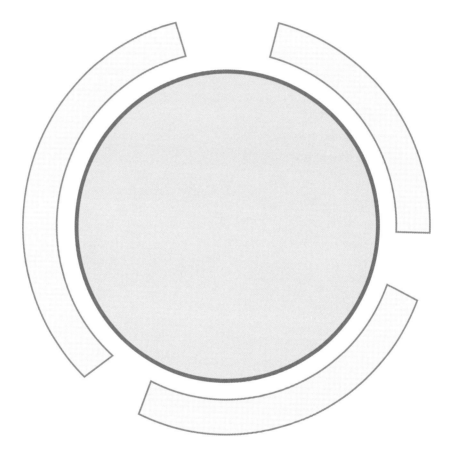

Acting with confidence doesn't mean you need to hide feelings of worry, fear or low confidence. When we express our feelings, talk about them and find comfort, they can move out of our body, making room for calm and confidence.

HELPING OUR EMOTIONS TO MOVE

Have you ever laid down outside and watched clouds drift across the sky? Emotions are a bit like clouds – they're there for a little while, then if we let them, they'll gently drift away.

Lots of people try to hide their emotions inside, as they think it'll help them be more confident. But it doesn't work! Emotions need to be felt and expressed in order to move them out of our bodies. If we squish them down inside ourselves, there's no room for calm feelings and confidence.

There are lots of ways we can express emotions on the outside. Here are the best ones for helping feelings move out of your body:

Talk to someone you trust: when we share our feelings with someone kind and understanding, we learn we are not alone with our feelings.

Move your body: stretch, jump, give yourself a hug – let yourself show how the emotion feels. It's your body's way of talking!

Write about or draw your feelings: you can let your feelings out using pens and pencils.

When you're facing a challenge and feeling worried, scared or any other difficult emotion, try doing one, two or all three of these things. You'll see they help the difficult feelings move out of your body.

Buzz loves to watch clouds drift across the sky. Can you spot all of these shapes in the clouds outside of your window?

☐ **Duck**
☐ **Speech bubble**
☐ **Heart**

☐ **Train**
☐ **Shark**

ACTIVITY: MY STRENGTHS

Can you think of ten of your strengths? You probably have loads more, but there's only room for ten here! Think about things you're good at, things that feel easy for you and nice things others notice about you. For example: I'm a kind friend, I have a wonderful imagination.

Recognizing your strengths helps build confidence – when you realize how awesome you already are, it gets easier to believe in yourself!

I LIKE MYSELF!

When you're a good friend to yourself, confidence grows. Take some time to draw a picture of yourself to celebrate you. Can you draw a self-portrait in the frame? Try looking at yourself in a mirror or photograph as a guide. You can draw your whole body or just your face – you choose!

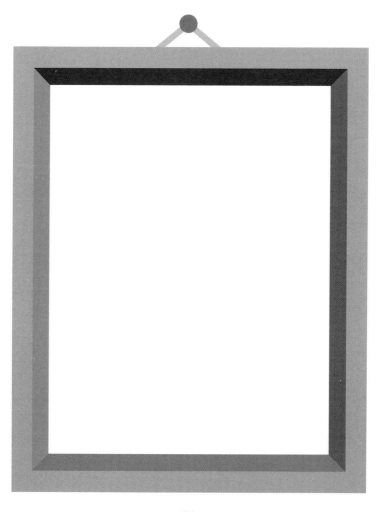

I LIKE
BEING ME

ACTIVITY: ONE STEP AT A TIME

When we focus on everything turning out perfectly – whether you're making a new friend, doing a spelling test or playing as part of a team – it's very hard to feel relaxed and confident. The truth is, we can't control how any experience unfolds, we can only control whether we do our best.

Instead of focusing on the top of your confidence staircase, slow down and concentrate on the next step ahead of you.

Here's Buzz's footprint – can you draw your footprint on the opposite page? You could trace around your foot or draw it.

Draw around your foot here:

Buzz's footprint looks quite different to yours, and that's OK – everybody's brave steps towards confidence are unique and special. Do your best at every step and you'll get to your goal!

ACTIVITY: CONFIDENT COLOURING

Colouring and drawing isn't just a fun and relaxing way to spend your time. It can also help you shift your thoughts towards more positive, confident ones. Because colouring engages your mind and your senses, colouring in a positive message (rather than just saying or reading it) helps your brain get more comfortable with believing it. Use your favourite coloured pens or pencils to decorate these words!

I can do my best

I've got this

My confidence is GROWING

SAYING NO

Confidence isn't just about saying yes to new things – sometimes the bravest thing we can do is say: "No, that's not right for me". Perhaps a friend has invited you to a theme park, or you've been offered a piece of cake but your tummy is full – it can feel difficult to say no, especially if we're worried about hurting someone's feelings.

It's OK for others to feel difficult feelings. Just like you, other people can feel all emotions.

There are lots of ways we can say "no" – here are a few to practise. Which ones feel good to say?

How about something else instead?

I'd really like to, but I can't.

That's not right for me.

I don't want to.

YOUR SECRET SUPERPOWER

Have you heard the word "empathy" before? Empathy means imagining what it might be like to be someone else, and what emotions they might be feeling. You might not know it yet, but it's a superpower for building confidence. Here's why.

When Buzz sees that their friend Jem has dropped an ice cream on the ground, Buzz uses empathy:

Using clues like Jem's facial expression, facts Buzz knows about Jem and imagining what it would be like to be Jem in that moment, Buzz has a good guess at how Jem is feeling.

A lot of the time, our brains use empathy without us having to think about it too much. But when you're feeling low on confidence, it can take a little effort to use these powers.

Instead of using clues and imagining ourselves as other people, we often think thoughts like:

When you use empathy, you realize that others are often feeling similar emotions and thinking similar thoughts to you.

If they're in the same situation as you, chances are you have a lot in common, even if it doesn't seem that way on the outside. When we use empathy, we can make the kindest, most generous guess at how others are feeling.

If you're in a different situation, think back to when you were in their shoes…

When you use your powers of empathy, you'll see it's a superpower for building confidence: it zaps away worries about what other people are thinking and feeling!

I AM
KIND

MAKING MISTAKES

There's nothing that brings our confidence down quite like worrying about making a mistake. It makes you freeze up and stops you before you even get going!

The truth is, mistakes are how we learn, and how we create and discover new things.

Did you know, all of these things were invented when someone made a mistake?

- Slime

- Superglue

- Sticky notes

- Potato chips

- Slinky springs

- Chocolate-chip cookies

When we focus on being perfect and avoiding mistakes, it's very hard to relax and simply do our best. Think of mistakes and accidents as experiments rather than disasters, and you'll find it's easier to go with the flow.

ACTIVITY: SCRIBBLE MAGIC!

Buzz is experimenting with drawing. With closed eyes, Buzz makes a scribble on the paper. With open eyes, Buzz transforms it into a picture!

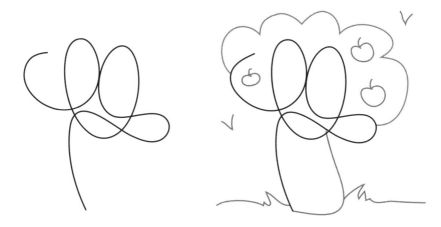

Can you transform Buzz's scribble into a picture?

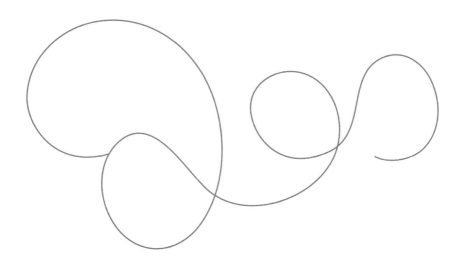

Why not try it yourself? Close your eyes and scribble on the page… then open your eyes and see what your scribble could become!

MY MOST CONFIDENT SELF

Think about when you feel most confident. Ask yourself these questions:

 Where am I?

Who am I with?

What am I wearing?

What am I doing?

How am I standing?

What do I say?

Use the answers you've come up with to draw or write about your most confident self on the opposite page.

Your confident self is inside you, all the time. It's just that sometimes you can feel it more strongly than others. Whenever you need a confidence boost, come back to this page and remind yourself of confident you.

My confident self looks like…

I AM GROWING IN CONFIDENCE EVERY DAY

IT'S OK TO FEEL HOW YOU FEEL

There's a lot of information about confidence in this book, and you might be wondering if you should be feeling confident all the time. Here's the good news – it's OK to feel exactly how you feel, at any moment.

Worrying that you are experiencing the "wrong" emotions or that you should feel the same as everybody else will bring your confidence down.

When we accept our feelings and remember that it's OK to feel them, we can relax and do our best – leaving more space for confidence!

ACTIVITY: HELP BUZZ GET CREATIVE

Today, Buzz's class is painting pictures. Buzz loves to paint but is worried about making a mistake. Buzz can't seem to begin painting!

What could you say to help Buzz think differently and build confidence, so Buzz can have fun and get creative?

PART 4:
LOOKING AFTER YOU

When we take good care of ourselves – eating well, drinking lots of water, getting plenty of rest and exercise, and getting out in the sunshine – we feel more confident. In this chapter, you'll find loads of ideas for taking great care of you!

WHY IS TAKING CARE OF OURSELVES IMPORTANT FOR CONFIDENCE?

When our bodies have everything they need, feeling confident is much easier. That's because if we haven't had enough sleep, for example, our bodies have less energy than usual, and we need to work harder to do things like brushing our teeth or chatting to friends.

If we have less energy to do things we're already used to, finding the bravery to face challenges and build confidence is even harder.

So when we take care of our basic needs, we feel as good and as energized as possible. When we feel great already, confidence is a lot easier to find.

CONFIDENCE-BUILDING FOOD

Eating plenty of healthy food will help your body feel great every day. Lots of fruit, vegetables, whole grains and protein – plus the odd treat here and there – will keep you energized and ready to face any challenges that come your way.

But did you know that cooking and preparing food is a huge confidence builder too? It's true! Cooking involves learning new skills and experimenting – plus you get something yummy to eat and share at the end. It's a brilliant confidence-building activity you can do at home.

On the next few pages, you'll find some great recipes to try. Always keep a grown-up nearby for any tricky bits – having support helps you learn new skills with confidence!

HOME-MADE PITTA PIZZA

Makes four mini pizzas

You will need:

- 2 pittas or 4 flatbreads
- 4 tbsp passata
- 250 g grated mozzarella

Method:

1. If you're using pittas, warm these gently in the toaster or under the grill until they puff up. This will take a minute or two.

2. Carefully split the pittas into two flat ovals. Be sure to wear oven gloves – the air inside gets very hot!

3. Place the pittas or flatbreads onto a baking tray, soft side up.

4. Spread passata onto each pitta, then add mozzarella and any other toppings you like.

5. Cook for 2–3 minutes under the grill until the mozzarella bubbles. Serve with a salad.

> **Confidence-building tip:** Why not try making a half-and-half pizza, with two different toppings? This will challenge your creativity and kitchen skills!

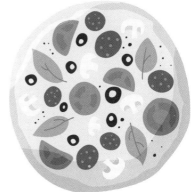

FROZEN YOGHURT BITES

Makes 12 bites

You will need:

- 200 g your favourite yoghurt – strawberry works well!

- Handful of fresh fruit – chopped strawberries, banana, kiwi, grapes, blueberries and raspberries are good options

- 12 silicone or paper cupcake cases

Method:

1. Begin by making sure there is space in your freezer. You'll need a tray or flat baking sheet that fits inside.

2. Lay out your cupcake cases and add a tablespoon of yoghurt to each one. Keep going until all the cake cases are full or all of your yoghurt is gone.

3. Add some fruit to the top of each.

4. Put the tray in the freezer and leave for two hours, until the yoghurt is frozen solid.

5. Pop the bites out of their cases and eat straight away or freeze them in a sealable plastic bag for later!

> **Confidence-building tip:** Try experimenting with different containers to make your frozen yoghurt bites, like an ice-cube tray, empty yoghurt pots or even a clean silicone bubble fidget toy! Which containers make the best bites?

FLUFFY BANANA BREAKFAST PANCAKES

Makes 12 pancakes

You will need:

- 350 g self-raising flour
- 1 tsp baking powder
- 2 ripe bananas (the spottier the better!)
- 2 eggs
- 250 ml milk
- Oil or butter for frying

Method:

1. Combine the flour and baking powder in a large mixing bowl.

2. In another bowl, mash the bananas with a fork until they're smooth, then stir in the eggs and milk.

3. Add the banana mixture to the flour and stir until they make a smooth batter.

4. Ask a grown-up to help you heat a little oil to a medium heat in a frying pan.

5. Add about 2 tbsp of batter to the pan to make each pancake. When you see little bubbles on the top of the batter, the pancake is ready to turn.

6. Let the other side cook for 1–2 minutes, keeping in mind that you won't be able to see any bubbles!

7. Repeat until you've used all your batter and serve the pancakes warm.

Confidence-building tip: It can take a few goes to get the temperature and timing just right, so your first few pancakes might not look how you'd like them to. Enjoy your less-than-perfect pancakes and practise being kind to yourself as you learn!

CONFIDENCE AND SLEEP

When we've had a good night's sleep, it's a lot easier to feel like our most confident selves and do brave things. But at the same time, it can be super difficult to fall asleep if you're feeling low in confidence.

To help solve this tricky problem, arm yourself with tools you can use when you need a little extra help falling asleep. Here's a brilliant one:

Relaxing from your toes to your head

1. Get ready to sleep, making sure you're nice and comfy in bed. Starting with your toes, you're going to relax every part of your body, one by one.

2. Stretch and wriggle your toes in any way that feels good – this will let the nervous energy out.

3. After a good wriggle, think about relaxing your toes, so they can fall asleep. This doesn't need to be perfect, just spend a few moments feeling your toes.

4. Repeat these steps with your feet, ankles, calves, knees… all the way to the top of your head.

This exercise helps focus your mind away from worries and relaxes your body at the same time. Hopefully, you'll fall asleep before you get to the top of your head, but if you don't, that's OK – you can keep going for as long as you like, this time from your head to your toes!

ACTIVITY: MOVE YOUR BODY!

When we feel nervous, worried or low in confidence, often we want to freeze, scrunch up small or even run away from our challenges.

We've learned quite a lot about how our thoughts can help us feel more confident, but it works the other way too – we can move our bodies in ways that help our emotions change, which in turn helps our thoughts become more confident. Our minds and bodies are always communicating with each other!

So, when you feel like you want to curl up small and still, you can try one of the movements on the next page to gently bring more confidence into your body.

Yoga poses to bring you confidence

Yoga is a form of exercise originating from India. Using stretches, deep breathing and gentle movement, it can bring calm and confidence to your body and mind. There are many different yoga poses. Here are just a few confidence-boosting poses for you to try:

Star pose

Spread your feet and arms wide, and look straight ahead to the horizon. Make your body as big as you can, and take three long, deep breaths.

Warrior pose

Stand straight and tall, then take a big step forward. Put your hands together and raise them up to the sky. Turn your back foot outward and bend your front knee. Feel your own strength and take three deep breaths, then switch sides and repeat.

Tree pose

Stand up straight and tall, and put your hands together. Find something tall and straight – like a tree – to look at; it'll help you balance. Now bring the sole of one foot up to rest on the opposite ankle. Take a deep breath. You can stay in this position or, if you're feeling steady, slowly bring your foot a little higher up your leg. When you find a good position that's challenging but not too wobbly, stay there for three breaths. Then switch legs and repeat.

I AM
STRONG

GO WILD

Getting out in nature is a brilliant (and fun) way to build confidence. Because there's always something new to discover, being out in nature helps us think, play and solve problems more creatively. Whether you're hunting for shells, finding your way around a muddy puddle or building a den, there are always big and small challenges to overcome – and when we overcome challenges, our confidence grows.

MAKE A NATURE MANDALA

A mandala is a spiritual, circular pattern that's symbolic in Buddhist and Hindu cultures. Mandalas can be drawn, painted, collaged or made by placing objects in a circle. Let's make a nature mandala with Buzz!

Buzz collects leaves, flowers and stones found on the ground at the park. Carefully, Buzz arranges them in a circle. When the mandala is finished, Buzz leaves it on the ground for someone else to find!

Next time you're out in nature, try making your own mandala. Take care to use natural objects you find on the ground, like…

Stones   Leaves   Flowers

Shells   Sticks

You can make a mandala at home, too. Here are some fun mandala ideas to inspire you:

MAKING TIME TO CHILL OUT

Building confidence and acting with bravery is tiring! Taking time to relax every day is like recharging your batteries, and it's really important for all sorts of reasons. Daily relaxation leads to:

- Better sleep

- Less anxiety

- Clearer thinking

Make time to do something relaxing every day. It could be reading, playing quietly, watching TV, dancing, drawing… however you like to chill out.

How will you relax each day this week? Plan your chill-out time using this handy planner:

	Chill-out time	Chill-out activity
Monday		
Tuesday		
Wednesday		
Thursday		
Friday		
Saturday		
Sunday		

CONFIDENCE-BUILDING FRIENDSHIPS

We need to spend time with others and nurture friendships in order to be healthy and calm. Good friendships build up our confidence because when we know our friends will be there for us whatever happens, we can find the bravery to face challenges.

Making friends takes bravery too, so it's OK if you find friendships difficult. Just one or two really good friends are much better than a hundred friends who don't properly know the real you.

WHAT MAKES A GOOD FRIEND?

Good friends build up each other's confidence, but bad friendships can bring it down. Look out for these signs of good and bad friendships:

A good friend...	A bad friend...
Shows kindness	Is mean to you
Gets to know you	Only thinks of themselves
Cares about your feelings	Doesn't mind hurting your feelings
Is someone you feel calm around	Is someone you feel worried or scared around
Spends time with you	Ignores you

If someone is behaving like a bad friend towards you, remember that it's not your fault. You are in charge of your actions, and they are in charge of theirs. You don't have to be friends with someone who treats you badly and hurts your confidence. If you need help dealing with a bad friendship, you can ask a trusted grown-up for support.

I AM A
GOOD FRIEND
TO MYSELF
AND OTHERS

ACTIVITY: MY GOOD FRIEND

Having just one good friend can make a huge difference to our confidence. Pick one good friend and fill in the blanks…

Draw your friend in the frame.

My good friend's name is...

My favourite memory together is...

I have known him/her/them since...

We're both interested in...

He/she/they make me feel...

BUILDING CONFIDENCE TOGETHER

How can good friends help build up each other's confidence? There are lots of ways! Here are just a few:

Celebrating each other's big and small wins

Getting to know each other well

Showing empathy

Listening and sharing feelings

Standing up for each other

Speaking to and about each other with kindness

Taking time to understand each other's strengths and challenges

Showing respect

Having fun together

Being trustworthy

Helping each other with challenges

Let's take a look at how we can build confidence with our friends together.

Buzz and Blip are in the same chess club. They are good friends, and they love spending time together.

Having fun together.

Taking time to understand each other's strengths and challenges.

Next week, Blip is going to play the teacher at chess. Even though the teacher is a kind, trusted grown-up, Buzz knows Blip is feeling really nervous!

Buzz helps Blip practise for the game, and they do some deep breathing together so Blip can feel as calm as possible.

Helping with challenges.

Showing empathy.

At the game, Buzz is there watching so Blip knows there's a good friend nearby.

After the game, Buzz and Blip celebrate Blip's bravery!

Celebrating big and small wins.

Being trustworthy.

Buzz feels inspired by Blip's bravery and knows Blip will be a good friend when Buzz is facing a challenge.

ACTIVITY: BUILDING INDEPENDENCE

Learning how to do things for ourselves and help others is a huge confidence builder. It boosts our self-worth and self-esteem when we can make a difference to the people around us at home, at school and in our communities.

Home is the best place to start building independence, so get together with your grown-up and pick a skill they can support you to learn. Here are a few to get you thinking, plus there's space to add your own ideas:

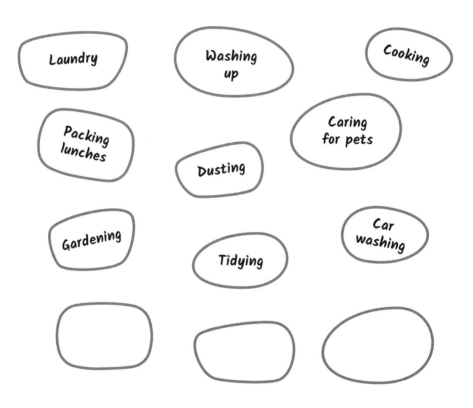

What did you and your grown-up pick? Use this confidence staircase to plan how you'll learn this new skill!

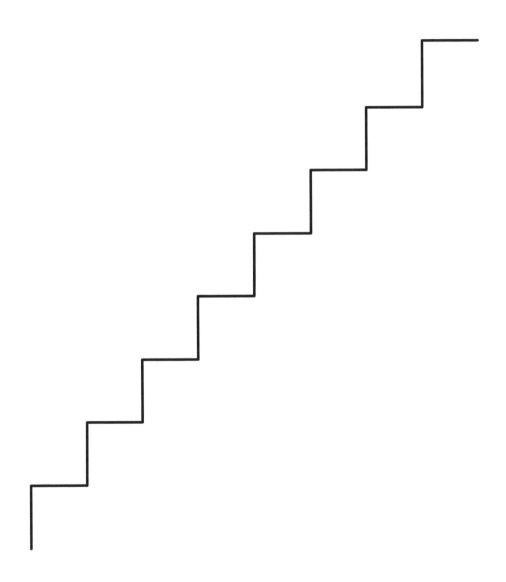

Once you've built up some confidence in your chosen skill, come back to this page! What's it like to learn this skill? Can you write or draw instructions for someone who's beginning to learn it?

I CAN
LEARN
NEW
SKILLS

BUILDING BODY CONFIDENCE

Some of us find it difficult to feel confident because we worry about what people think about how we look. Perhaps we've heard unkind words used about our bodies, or about other people who look like we do.

One way to build confidence in ourselves and our bodies is to show ourselves gratitude. When we look for positives about ourselves, feeling good about ourselves becomes easier. Let's try it!

Now it's your turn – what do you feel grateful for today?

FEED YOUR MIND GOOD THINGS

Our brains are always hungry for information, and they eat up information all day long! Whether it's a new fact, an interesting idea or an unkind opinion, our brains take in the things we see and hear.

We can't stop our brains from taking in the things that lower our confidence, but we can take the time to feed our brains positive, confidence-building information to make up for it. One quick and clever way is by using positive affirmations.

Affirmations are short sentences designed to be read aloud or in our heads. When we read them, they work to help us feel good! Here are some confidence-boosting affirmations.

Why not carefully cut out these affirmations, and stick them somewhere you'll see them every day?

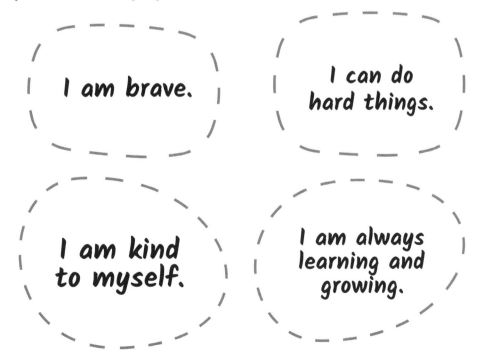

I am brave.

I can do hard things.

I am kind to myself.

I am always learning and growing.

PART 5: QUICK CONFIDENCE BOOSTERS

We've learned a lot about facing challenges one step at a time – it's the best way to build long-lasting confidence. But it takes time, and sometimes you need a dose of confidence quickly! This chapter is all about the tricks and hacks that can give you that boost.

BREATHING IN CONFIDENCE

There are times when we might need to find confidence in a hurry – like if a friend is being bullied and we need to stand up for them, or if we want to start a conversation with a potential new friend. When this happens, we usually don't have time to work out our brave steps or do a few calming yoga stretches. Luckily, there's one confidence-boosting, anxiety-calming tool that's always available to us – our breath!

We breathe in and out all day and night, and 99 per cent of the time we don't think about it. When we're feeling anxious and low on confidence, our breathing can get fast and shallow, which brings less oxygen into our bodies.

When we have less oxygen in our bodies, feelings of anxiety and low confidence get worse. So, taking a moment to change how we're breathing will help our bodies to feel better, our emotions to shift and our confidence to rise.

A simple slow, deep breath in and out will help – take as many as you need until you feel a difference. You can also try breathing exercises to super-charge your breath's confidence-boosting powers. You'll find two breathing exercises on the next pages, which you can try anywhere!

Bubble breathing

Use the power of your imagination to slow your breathing and increase your confidence! Here's how:

1. Take a slow, deep breath in and out to prepare.

2. Take a deep breath in.

3. Breathe out through your mouth, imagining you are blowing a bubble. The longer you exhale, the bigger the bubble grows.

4. When you're ready to breathe in again, let the bubble go. Imagine it floating up or bobbing around near you – whichever feels best.

5. With your next breath, blow another huge bubble.

6. Keep going for five breaths.

Shoulder-roll breathing

This exercise helps you release tension and stand tall. Here's how to do it:

1. Take a deep breath in and out to prepare.

2. Take a deep breath in, raising your shoulders up toward your ears.

3. As you breathe out, bring your shoulders back and down, as far from your ears as you can.

4. Keep going for five breaths, in and out.

When you're finished, relax your shoulders down away from your ears. Holding your body in this way will help you feel a little calmer, braver and more confident.

ACTIVITY: MY CONFIDENCE FILE

Our brains often find it a lot easier to remember unkind, confidence-lowering words and experiences than kind, confidence-boosting ones. For this reason, it's useful to collect positive memories and words in a confidence file!

You will need:

- 1 large envelope
- Paper
- Scissors
- Pens and/or pencils

Method:

1. Decorate your envelope like a top-secret file. This is where you'll keep your most powerful confidence-boosting words – it's important to keep them safe!

2. Cut out squares of paper and write or draw the things that make you feel confident. You can include:

   - Kind words others have said to you
   - Things you're already really good at
   - Times when things have gone really well
   - Achievements you're proud of

3. Ask your friends and trusted grown-ups to write confidence-boosting notes for you.

4. Keep your confidence file somewhere safe and take a look inside whenever you need a lift.

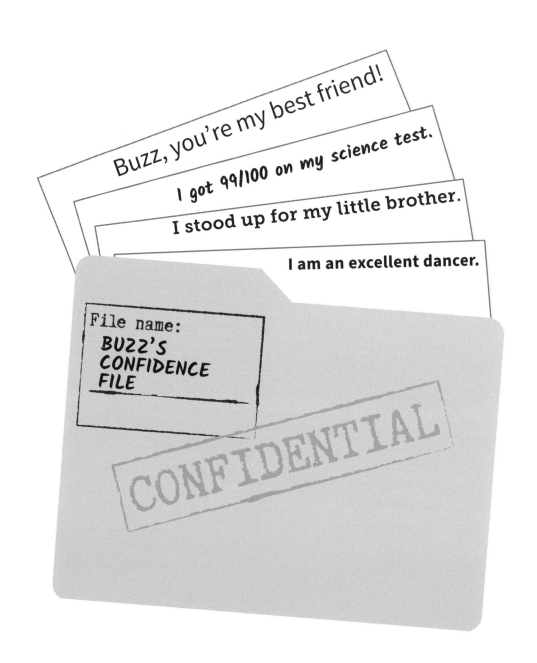

Buzz, you're my best friend!

I got 99/100 on my science test.

I stood up for my little brother.

I am an excellent dancer.

File name:
BUZZ'S
CONFIDENCE
FILE

CONFIDENTIAL

I AM
COURAGEOUS

HOW GRATITUDE BOOSTS CONFIDENCE

When we feel low on confidence, our minds start to notice all the negatives and obstacles in our way, and it gets hard to see the positives in a situation.

One of Buzz's favourite authors is visiting school today! Buzz really wants to ask her a question, but this feels really scary when Buzz thinks about it.

Did you notice how Buzz's brain was thinking about all the negative things that could happen? When we use gratitude, we take a moment to look for positives – even if they're small. Buzz uses gratitude for a boost of confidence:

Even though Buzz still feels nervous, finding three things to be grateful for gives Buzz a boost! Now it feels a bit easier to find bravery.

ACTIVITY: GRATITUDE CHALLENGES!

Buzz's quick gratitude practice helped Buzz find positivity and bravery. Now it's your turn! Can you complete the gratitude challenges?

Three people or animals I'm grateful for...

Three foods I'm grateful for...

Three things in my home I'm grateful for...

Three books, games, films or TV shows I'm grateful for...

Three memories I'm grateful for...

SHAKING OFF ANXIETY

Moving our bodies helps tension and difficult emotions move through and out, leaving space for us to feel calm and confident. We learned about yoga stretches on page 92, and here you'll find some even quicker ways to move anxiety out of your body.

Shake it off

Wriggle your hips, jiggle your feet and shake your arms. Do whatever feels best! Moving in this way will help loosen up your muscles, releasing tension and anxiety.

Stomp your feet

Imagine sending your anxious feelings deep into the earth as you stomp your feet with all your might.

Dance, dance, dance!

Play some music and dance – it's fun and will help lift your mood.

March to the beat of your own drum

Drum your hands on your body to make a tune. The rhythmic sounds and movement help calm anxious thoughts and feelings.

SPEAK YOURSELF CONFIDENT

Repeating positive affirmations to ourselves helps shift our thoughts and feelings towards confidence and positivity. Try saying these affirmations to yourself and see how they feel:

Did you have a favourite affirmation on the last page? A sentence that made you feel a little more positive and confident? Write it in big letters here!

When we repeat affirmations to ourselves – out loud or in our heads – our brains begin to believe them. Challenge yourself to repeat your favourite affirmation three times today!

THE BEST THAT CAN HAPPEN

Low confidence makes us imagine the worst. Take a moment to imagine the very best happening and see how it feels.

It's Buzz's first time playing on the basketball team. Buzz feels low on confidence and is imagining everything going wrong!

Buzz takes a deep breath and imagines a positive outcome.

Most of the time, things turn out somewhere in the middle... not the best and not the worst. Our brains like to think they know what the future holds, but in reality, they don't. We can imagine things that lower our confidence, or things that build it up. Next time you need a boost, take a moment to close your eyes and imagine a positive, confident outcome.

ANYTHING
IS POSSIBLE

PART 6: LOOKING FORWARD

You've reached the final chapter! We've learned so much about how confidence works, about skills for building that confidence and how to be kind to ourselves. Now it's time to put it into practice. In this chapter, we'll look at using our new confidence tools in the real world.

GOLDEN RULES FOR CONFIDENCE

Go at your own pace.

Be a good friend
to yourself.

Share your feelings with
trusted friends and
grown-ups.

Take good care of
your body and mind.

Take one step at a
time to build strong
confidence.

YOU ARE NOT ALONE

Everybody struggles with confidence sometimes – even people who appear to be super confident. Here are some stories of kids just like you:

> *My friend and I went ice skating – she's pretty good at it. I'd never been ice skating before, and I thought I'd just hold onto the side while she skated around – I didn't want to ruin her fun. But she held my hand and showed me how to find my balance. We both fell over loads of times, but knowing we would help each other up gave me so much confidence.*

Isla, 10

> *A group of my friends were making fun of another boy in our class while he wasn't there. I didn't like it and didn't want to join in. When one of them asked me why I wasn't laughing, I took a deep breath and told them what they were doing wasn't cool. It felt scary but I'm glad I spoke up.*

Omar, 9

> *I got the chance to go to a forest school – it was so cool. We learned how to build a fire safely and cooked pancakes over it. I wanted to show my mum, and we made a little campfire in our garden. It felt really good to teach a grown-up something!*

Noah, 8

" I was having trouble with my maths homework. Neither of my parents could understand it either, and I was getting quite frustrated. I worried that I'd get into trouble if I didn't get all the answers right, but I just couldn't do it! In the end, I sent a message to my teacher explaining that it didn't make sense to me. He was really understanding. Next lesson, he took the time to explain the homework in more detail. It turned out lots of kids hadn't been able to do it! "

Edie, 11

" My grandparents are from Hungary. My dad taught me and my brother some words in Hungarian, but I felt too shy and couldn't get my voice loud enough. My dad said it was OK, speaking another language is hard, and that trying my best was really great. The next time they came to stay, I said "*Szia*", which means "Hello", in a quiet voice. My grandparents were so excited, they loved hearing me try my best and it felt easier to show them the other words I've learned. "

Hanna, 7

" I started a new school this year and one day I couldn't find my classroom. I looked for a teacher but couldn't find one, and I was getting even more lost! I felt embarrassed and worried that the other kids would laugh at me if they knew, but I stood tall and asked a friendly-looking kid. He was really kind and walked me to my classroom. He showed me that it's worth asking for help, even when it's hard. "

Ryan, 11

SPREADING RIPPLES OF CONFIDENCE

When you act with bravery, kindness and confidence, it spreads! Think about how inspired you are when others act with confidence. You can be that person for others, inspiring friends and loved ones with your positive actions and helping their confidence grow.

When you drop a pebble into a pool of water, it creates ripples on the surface that spread. It doesn't matter if your pebble is only very small, it still has an effect.

Each time you act with bravery, colour in one of the pebbles below. Here are some ideas to get you started, and blank pebbles for you to add your own.

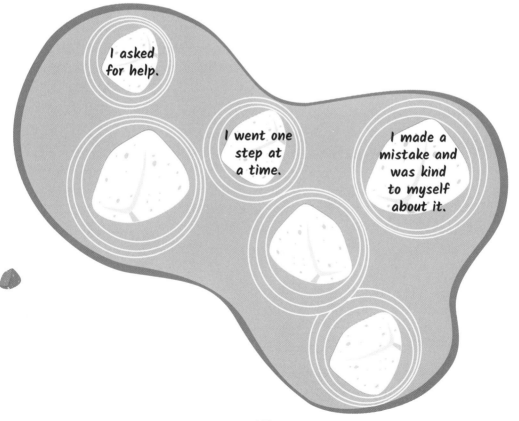

ACTIVITY:
MAKE A CONFIDENCE-BUILDING POSTER

What would you say to someone struggling with low confidence? Think about what words would help you feel brave and write them on this poster. You can colour in and decorate the poster in whatever way you'd like. When you're ready, carefully cut it out.

Put your poster somewhere others will see it. It could be facing outward on your window, on a noticeboard at school or even in a library book for someone to find.

THE END!

You've reached the end of the book! Buzz has had an amazing time learning all about confidence with you! Have you had a good time, too? Remember: you can always come back to this book if you need a boost of confidence, to remind yourself how strong and capable you are or to share the ideas with a friend.

You've done so well – be very proud of yourself! Building confidence isn't easy, and you're doing it your way: that's pretty awesome!

I HAVE CONFIDENCE!

For parents and carers:
Ways you can support your child's confidence

True confidence looks different on everyone. It's possible your child will develop a love of public speaking or being the centre of attention, but it's important to recognize that there are lots of different ways to act with confidence. Whether it's speaking up when they don't understand a question at school, having a tricky conversation with a friend or trying a new activity, confidence and bravery come in many forms.

You know your child better than anybody, so you'll know what they find challenging, and you're perfectly placed to see those quiet triumphs that others might not notice. Showing your child that you appreciate their inner world and that you're keen to understand them more deeply will make a huge difference to their ability to build confidence.

When children feel sure that you are always on their team, that you will treat their wins with pride and their losses with gentleness, it becomes easier for them to take leaps of faith towards their challenges. One of the worst things about trying and failing is the feeling that you are alone with the difficult emotions failure brings. You can be there to show your child they are definitely not alone.

In practical terms, this could look like giving voice to anxiety your child feels unable to mention or finding creative ways to support your child in facing their challenges. For example, a dreaded exam could be made less anxiety-provoking by studying together, finding fun in the topic or sharing your own experiences of exam stress.

Whatever the challenge, going at a pace that feels comfortable for your child is the very best way to build confidence. When something feels like a huge mountain, breaking it down into more manageable steps makes the journey feel infinitely more relaxed and achievable.

I do hope this book has been helpful for you and your child. It's not easy to see them struggling. You're doing a great job by supporting them to build their confidence in a steady, sustainable way. Your child is lucky to have you on their team!

Further advice

If you're worried about your child's mental health, do talk it through with your doctor. While almost all children experience emotional ups and downs, some may benefit from extra support. There are lots of great resources out there for information and guidance on children's mental health. Here are just a few:

YoungMinds Parents' Helpline (UK)
www.youngminds.org.uk
0808 802 5544

BBC Bitesize (UK)
www.bbc.co.uk/bitesize/support

Childline (UK)
www.childline.org.uk
0800 1111

Child Mind Institute (USA)
www.childmind.org

The Youth Mental Health Project (USA)
www.ymhproject.org

Recommended reading

For children:

Ella on the Outside by Cath Howe
Nosy Crow, 2018

You Are Awesome: Find Your Confidence and Dare to be Brilliant at (Almost) Anything by Matthew Syed
Wren & Rook, 2018

Wreck This Journal by Keri Smith
Penguin, 2013

For adults:

The Book You Wish Your Parents Had Read (and Your Children Will be Glad That You Did) by Philippa Perry
Penguin Life, 2020

The Story Cure: An A–Z of Books to Keep Kids Happy, Healthy and Wise by Ella Berthoud and Susan Elderkin
Canongate Books, 2017

Happy High Status: How to Be Effortlessly Confident by Viv Groskop
Torva, 2023

Credits

Other books in the series...

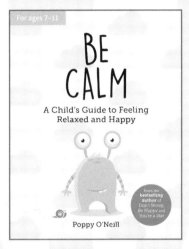

Paperback
ISBN: 978-1-80007-711-9

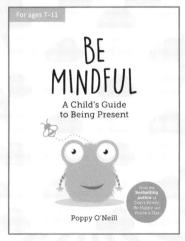

Paperback
ISBN: 978-1-80007-710-2

Have you enjoyed this book?
If so, why not write a review on your favourite website?

If you're interested in finding out more about our books,
find us on Facebook at **Summersdale Publishers,**
on Twitter/X at **@Summersdale** and on Instagram
and TikTok at **@summersdalebooks** and get in touch.
We'd love to hear from you!

Thanks very much for buying this Summersdale book.

www.summersdale.com